TEN GREAT AFRICAN AMERICAN MEN OF SCIENCE

with Hands-On Activity Sheets

by Dr. Clifford Watson
Principal,
Malcolm X African American Academy
Detroit, Michigan

The Peoples Publishing Group, Inc.

Free to Learn, to Grow, to Change

1-800-822-1080

ILLUSTRATIONS: **Anita Temares**
PHOTO RESEARCH: **Daniel Ortiz, Jr.**
PRODUCTION: **BBE Associates, Ltd. & Doreen Smith**

Photo Credits: pp. 1, 8, 14, 18, 38, 71, The Peoples Publishing Group, Inc. Photo Archives; p. 28, Courtesy of Energy Innovations, Inc.; p. 47, The Western Reserve Historical Society, Cleveland, Ohio; p. 55, Courtesy of Dr. Alvin F. Poussaint Archives; pp. 64, 78, Photographs and Prints Division, Schomburg Center for Research in Black Culture, The New York Public Library, Astor, Lenox, and Tilden Foundations.

ISBN 1-56256-700-4

© 1995 by
The Peoples Publishing Group, Inc.
230 W. Passaic Street
Maywood, NJ 07607

Printed in the United States of America.

9 8 7 6 5 4 3

Contents

Safety First

This book contains various experiments that demonstrate the concepts studied during the careers of *Ten Great African American Men of Science.* **Safety First** is the most important guideline when completing any science activity.

Before You Begin This Book

1. Review this page of safety guidelines. Study the safety symbols. Find an example of each symbol in the book and read the safety instructions.

2. Make sure you know where to find the following items in your lab. Learn how to use them.
   - first-aid kit
   - fire extinguisher and fire blanket
   - protective masks, goggles, and aprons
   - emergency exits
   - telephone, to call for help.

3. Check to see that all containers are labeled so you know what substances they hold.

Safety Symbols & Instructions

When you see the following symbols, you will find instructions on how to work safely during a lab activity.

 Danger from living things

 Physical danger

 Protect your clothing

 Be careful using heat

 Electricity is dangerous

 Be careful with sharp objects

 Protect your eyes

Before You Experiment

1. Read the instructions for each *Hands-on Activity Sheet* before you begin. Review the safety symbols and instructions so that special safety equipment is ready before you start.

2. Wash all the tools you will use.

3. Make sure your teacher or another adult is present to supervise your work.

4. If your hair is long, wear a hair net or tie your hair back.

During An Experiment

5. Never run in a lab or play games during an experiment.

6. Do not bring food or drink into the lab or classroom.

7. Substances used in experiments can be dangerous. Only taste them or smell them if your teacher tells you to.

8. Mix ingredients only as a *Hands-on Activity Sheet* instructs. Playing with these ingredients may create dangerous or explosive substances.

9. Remember, knives and scissors are sharp. Move the knife or scissors away from your body when you cut anything.

10. Accidents do occur. Someone may be hurt or something may be broken. Immediately tell your teacher or the adult supervising your work.

11. To avoid a cut, use a broom and dustpan to clean up anything that breaks.

After The Experiment Is Done

12. Ask your teacher what to do with unused ingredients and containers.

13. Clean up your work area.

14. Make sure you turn off all lights, switches, burners, and faucets.

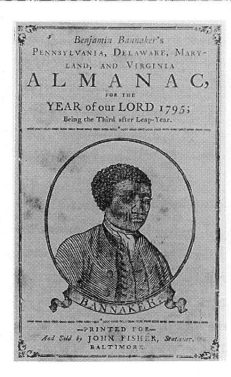

Chapter 1:
BENJAMIN BANNEKER
(November 9, 1731–October 9, 1806)
Inventor
Astronomer
Surveyor
Mathematician

☆ Benjamin Banneker was born in 1731.

☆ Benjamin Banneker was born a free man at a time when slavery was on the rise in Great Britain's colonies in America.

☆ Benjamin Banneker was a mathematician, astronomer, surveyor, and inventor.

☆ Benjamin Banneker wrote many articles against slavery.

☆ Benjamin Banneker built the first wooden clock made in America. He carved it by hand. He made the entire clock, including the running parts inside.

☆ Benjamin Banneker wrote an almanac in 1792 which was published in 1795.

☆ Banneker was one of the first African American men to write a letter to a U.S. president defending the intellectual capacities of African American people.

☆ In addition to being an outstanding astronomer and mathematician, Banneker was also a skilled surveyor. His survey was used to develop major buildings and much of our nation's capital, Washington, D.C.

☆ Benjamin Banneker died in 1806.

Benjamin Banneker

Benjamin Banneker was an African American scientist who demonstrated his scientific and mathematical genius to the world. Even though Banneker received little formal education, he taught himself. With the help of his mentor, Josef Levi, Banneker built the first wooden clock in America. Banneker used pictures of clocks and geometry books that Levi sent him from London. Banneker studied these, taught himself, and planned his clock. When it was built, people came from all across the country to see his clock!

By studying astronomy books and using some scientific instruments, Benjamin Banneker was able to accurately predict some important events. One of his most important predictions was a solar eclipse. Banneker's prediction was different from two well-known white scientists of the time. But Banneker's prediction about the time of the solar eclipse was right.

A solar eclipse takes place when the moon passes between the sun and the Earth. When this occurs, the moon casts a shadow on the Earth. If you ever observe an eclipse, notice whether it is a complete or partial eclipse. To see a complete, or total, eclipse, you must be standing on the part of Earth completely covered by the moon's shadow. A total eclipse of the sun is very dark. You see nothing but a small ring of light called a corona around the sun. The rest of the sun appears to be completely dark. This is caused by the moon's umbra, which is the totally dark center of its shadow.

You will see a solar eclipse as a partial eclipse when you are standing in a spot that is only partly inside the moon's umbra. The moon blocks out sunlight from only one part of the sun. Darkness occurs wherever the umbra touches Earth. Places at the edge of the eclipse are in the moon's penumbra, which is a ring of partial shadow around the moon's umbra. Since the penumbra is a partial shadow, there is dim light in these areas.

To record his scientific investigation and predictions, Banneker wrote an almanac in 1792. It contained information about weather forecasts for the year and the time of the eclipse, the hour of sunrise and sunset, festival days, phases of the moon, and other facts.

Benjamin Banneker did many great things at a time before Africans in the United States were allowed to go to school. He refused to be held back from achieving.

Safety Caution
Looking directly at a solar eclipse will damage your eyes. Use glasses or goggles that have been specially smoked or darkened. You can also punch a hole in a piece of cardboard. Then turn your back to the eclipse. Hold the cardboard in front of a piece of white paper. The eclipse's shadow passes through the hole and can be seen on the paper.

Benjamin Banneker

You Will Need:

- flashlight
- styrofoam ball, 1/2 inch to 1 inch (1.27 to 2.54 centimeters) in diameter
- white cardboard, at least 6 inches (15.24 centimeters) square
- household tape
- string

In this activity, you will demonstrate an umbra, which is the darker part of a shadow, and a penumbra, which is the lighter part of a shadow. In a solar eclipse, you cannot see the sun because the moon blocks its light. In a solar eclipse, the moon passes between the sun and the earth, creating a shadow. A shadow is the lack of light because light is blocked out.

Solar Eclipse

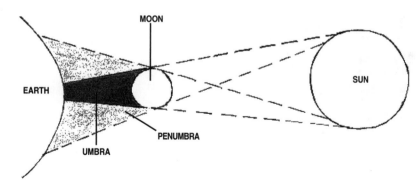

When there is an eclipse of the moon, or a lunar eclipse, the Earth is between the moon and the sun, blocking the light.

Lunar Eclipse

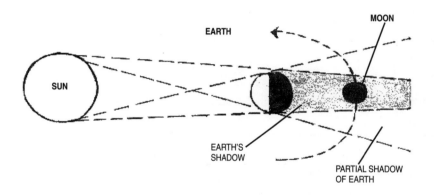

The kinds of shadows that cause eclipses of the sun and moon are called umbras and penumbras. You can demonstrate umbra and penumbra shadows in your classroom.

Safety Caution
Be careful not to burn yourself on the bulb while you are using the flashlight.

1. Darken the room.

2. Tape the cardboard to the wall.

3. Have one student shine the flashlight onto the cardboard.

4. Another student should tape the string around the styrofoam ball. Then, hold the ball between the flashlight and the cardboard.

5. Observe where the shadows fall.

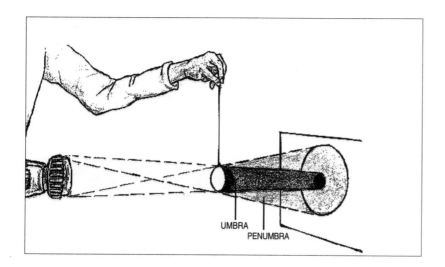

UMBRA
PENUMBRA

Record Your Observations:

1. Do you see a dark shadow? _____

   What is it called? _____

2. Do you see a light shadow? _____

   What is it called? _____

Draw Your Conclusions:

3. Explain in your own words how an eclipse happens. _____

_____

_____

_____

Benjamin Banneker

You Will Need:

- a picture of Benjamin Banneker for each student
- glue
- 2 pieces of cardboard, about 6 inches (15.24 centimeters) square
- scissors
- one brad
- magazines
- marker for writing
- paper

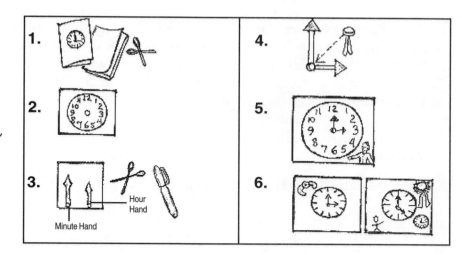

Benjamin Banneker built the first wooden clock in America. Mr. Banneker carved his clock from wood, using ideas from his mentor. You can design your clock from magazine pictures or from your own drawings.

1. Cut out 3–5 pictures of watches and clocks from magazines. If you do not want to use these pictures for your clock's face, design your own clock face on a separate piece of paper.

2. Draw your design or glue your picture onto a piece of cardboard. Mark the hours around the edge. Punch a small hole in the center of the face.

3. Cut out minute and hour hands from the other piece of cardboard. Punch a small hole in the end of each hand.

4. Use a brad to attach the hands to the hole in the center of the clock. Make sure the hands can move.

5. Banneker's picture can be glued at the bottom of the clock, or added to the design anywhere you wish.

6. Have a contest, and give a certificate or ribbon for the best-designed Banneker clock. Display the clocks.

My Thoughts about Benjamin Banneker:

_____

_____

_____

Note This activity should be done for students in the lower grades. Older students can make this clock for their younger brothers and sisters. Or, use this as a mentoring activity, pairing older and younger students.

Safety Caution
Be careful not to cut yourself with the scissors or the brad.

Benjamin Banneker

Write an essay about the eclipse of 1994. First, go to the library and do some research. Then, explain the significance of the eclipse of 1994. Give an explanation of times associated with the eclipse. Talk about the importance of predicting eclipses and other events, as Benjamin Banneker did in his almanac.

_____

_____

_____

_____

_____

_____

_____

_____

_____

_____

_____

_____

_____

_____

_____

_____

_____

_____

_____

Benjamin Banneker

Match the words from the list below with their correct meanings. Write each word on the line by its meaning.

eclipse	partial eclipse	inventor
total eclipse	almanac	corona
surveyor	umbra	astronomer
penumbra		

_____ 1. the blocking out of one heavenly body by another

_____ 2. a partial shadow

_____ 3. a yearly publication including calendars with weather forecasts, astronomical information, and other related information

_____ 4. the center of a shadow that blocks all light

_____ 5. the complete blocking out of one heavenly body by another

_____ 6. the bright light that appears to surround the sun during a total eclipse caused by the moon

_____ 7. a person who determines the boundaries and areas of land surfaces with the use of certain pieces of equipment

_____ 8. one who makes or designs new things

_____ 9. a person who studies heavenly bodies

_____ 10. the partial blocking out of one heavenly body by another

Chapter 2:
GEORGE WASHINGTON CARVER
(1864–January 5, 1943)
Agriculturalist
Scientist

☆ Dr. Carver was born a slave on a farm in Missouri.

☆ Dr. Carver was an outstanding agricultural scientist.

☆ Dr. Carver was an excellent artist. One of his paintings won honorable mention at the Chicago World's Fair in 1894. London's Royal Society of Arts invited Dr. Carver to join their organization in 1916.

☆ Dr. Carver made many products from the soybean, the sweet potato and the peanut. He made such items as flour, vinegar, shoe polish, molasses, starch, coffee, and almost a hundred other products from the sweet potato. From the peanut he made such things as metal polish, vegetable milk, ink, grease, cooking oils, peanut butter, and cheese. This work earned Dr. Carver the Spingarn Medal in 1923 and the Theodore Roosevelt Medal in 1939.

☆ Dr. Carver spent his entire life doing research and teaching at Tuskegee Institute in Alabama.

☆ Dr. Carver was appointed collaborator in mycology, the study of fungi, for the United States Department of Agriculture in 1934.

☆ Dr. Carver died in 1943.

☆ Dr. Carver's birthplace in Missouri became the George Washington Carver National Monument in 1951.

![barcode decoration]

George Washington Carver

In his early years of research, Dr. George Washington Carver studied fungi and molds. He wanted to know why they caused diseases in plants.

Have you ever left bread in a dark moist place for awhile? What happened? Did you notice a green growth on the bread? The growth you found is a common type of fungus called bread mold.

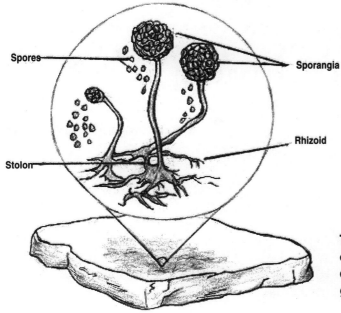

The bread mold fungus grows on bread. Never eat bread or any food with a fungus growing on it.

1. As each spore head of fungus falls on the bread, a new mold fungus begins to grow.

2. As the mold grows, the hyphae (HI-fee), or root-like growths, draw food substances up to the head of the fungus.

3. As the mold grows and spreads, the bread is eaten away and destroyed.

COMMON TYPES OF FUNGI

There are many different types of fungi. The ones that you are probably most familiar with are mushrooms, puffballs, and molds.

You may have seen mushrooms growing in your backyard or along a road, especially after a rain. You may have been tempted to sample some mushrooms. However, not all mushrooms are safe to eat, so you should not pick and eat them. There are several types of poisonous mushrooms. Each year many people die from eating poisonous mushrooms.

Many common mushrooms are edible and you may have seen them in the grocery store. These kinds of mushrooms are grown in pastures and meadows throughout the United States and Europe. There are thousands of different types of mushrooms.

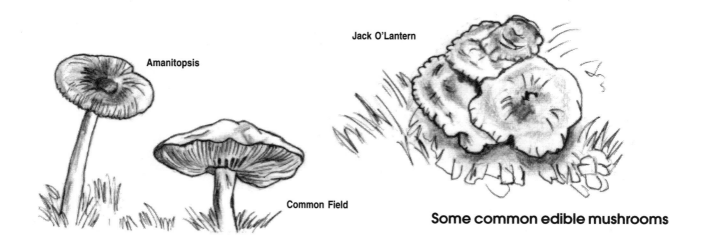

Amanitopsis

Jack O'Lantern

Common Field

Some common edible mushrooms

Another type of fungus is the puffball. Most puffballs are shaped like white balls. They are a large fungus. Puffballs can weigh up to 10 pounds. Puffballs grow in open fields. Some types of puffballs are edible.

Molds are another type of fungus. The kinds of molds that grow on bread are called bread molds or black molds, since most of the spores produced turn black in color.

a puffball fungus

Not all molds are harmful. There is one particular type of mold that produces the life-saving drug penicillin. Penicillin is an antibiotic and kills infections. Another type of common mold ripens roquefort cheese. Many molds are beneficial. Some break off waste matter. Some help in fertilizing the soil.

In the early 1900s, people in the South called the cotton plant king because it was their living. Cotton was the main cash crop. Then, an insect called the boll weevil destroyed much of the cotton crop. People were devastated.

a peanut plant

a peanut

It was Dr. George Washington Carver who came to the rescue with his inventive genius as an agriculturalist. An agriculturalist is a scientist who develops better ways to raise crops and livestock. Dr. Carver found that when the same crops were planted in a field year after year, the crops used up all the nutrients in the soil. After several years, the crop would not grow. This was devastating to farmers until Dr. Carver introduced the idea of crop rotation. By planting different crops in different years, farmers could keep the soil rich and fertile.

DR. CARVER'S LEGUMES

Dr. Carver also studied legumes, such as the peanut. Legumes are plants that grow seeds in pods. Dr. Carver began studying legumes in his research on crop rotation, or planting different crops in different years to keep the soil healthy.

You have probably eaten peanuts, but not really thought about what a peanut is. Actually, a peanut comes from the peanut plant, just as a pea comes from the pea plant. There can be two to five peanuts in a shell.

USES OF THE PEANUT

Peanuts are a good food source, and they taste good, too. Peanut butter is made by grinding peanuts into a pasty substance. Peanuts can also be roasted, cracked open, and eaten. Peanut oil is used for cooking.

Peanuts have many important uses. In industry, the oil from peanuts is used to lubricate machinery. The shells of the peanut are used to make powder, plastics, and wallboard. Farmers use peanut shells for cattle feed. They also use peanut shells as fertilizer.

HOW A PEANUT GROWS

A peanut plant starts off as a seed. It then grows into a plant and flowers. The flower grows for awhile and then falls off. What remains after the top part of the flower falls off is a fertilized base. This fertilized base begins to grow, forming a peg-like stem that pushes into the ground. Once in the ground, the peg grows into a peanut pod.

The majority of the world's peanuts are produced on the African and Asian continents. But many peanuts are now grown in the United States. And, thanks to Dr. Carver, peanuts are only one industry that makes the South successful.

George Washington Carver

You Will Need:

- *Morgan lepitotas* mushrooms, one per student, or any nonpoisonous mushrooms with gills
- a white piece of paper
- a knife for cutting the mushroom

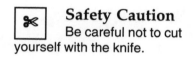

Safety Caution
Be careful not to cut yourself with the knife.

A beautiful spore picture can be made from a simple mushroom.

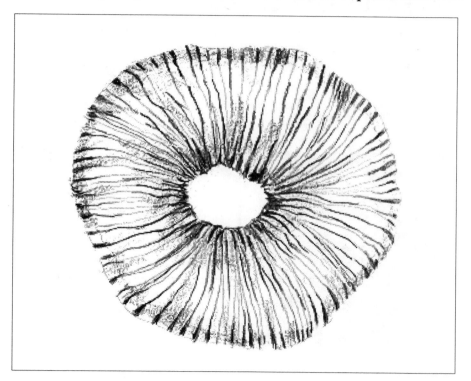

1. Cut off the stem of the mushroom. Be careful to cut down and away from yourself.

2. Turn the mushroom upside down and press it onto the white paper. Leave it there overnight.

3. The gills of the *lepitotas* tend to produce pink or green colors. If you are using another mushroom, the color may be different.

TEN GREAT AFRICAN AMERICAN MEN OF SCIENCE

George Washington Carver

You Will Need:

✄ **Safety Caution**
Be careful not to cut yourself with the scissors.

- to do research and list products that came from the peanut
- a large piece of heavy paper
- magazines
- scissors
- paints, pencils, and other drawing equipment

Safety Caution
Be sure to protect your clothing while working with paints.

CARVER PEANUT PRODUCT BOARD

	DR. CARVER	

---

1. Using a large piece of cardboard or a regular size bulletin board, make your own Carver Product Display.

2. Bring or draw pictures of some of the more than 325 different products that Dr. George Washington Carver developed from the peanut.

3. Paint or draw your pictures on sheets of white paper of equal size.

4. Attach your pictures to the squares on the cardboard.

George Washington Carver

You Will Need:

- 2 jars
- household tape
- paper
- scissors
- water
- 2 pieces of bread, 4 inches (10.16 centimeters) square, one dried out
- eyedropper
- a microscope, if available
- 2 slides

Does moisture cause a mold to grow?

1. Cut out two paper strips, 1 inch x 3 inches (2.54 centimeters x 7.62 centimeters) each. Label one strip as *Jar A* and the other strip as *Jar B*. Tape a label on each jar.

2. Take a dried-out piece of bread and one fresh piece of bread. The dried-out piece of bread will be a control sample. Place it in *Jar A*.

3. Place the second piece of bread in *Jar B*. Add a small amount of water to the jar.

4. Place both jars in a dark area. After 3 or 4 days, check both jars to see if any mold has formed.

5. The teacher will place a sample from each jar on slides. Use a lens or microscope to examine both samples.

Note The *control* in an experiment is the main sample to which the other samples are compared. For example, in this experiment you cannot tell what difference moisture makes in growing mold if you don't know *how* or even *if* mold grows in dry conditions.

Record Your Observations:

1. What did the mold samples look like? _____

_____

2. Did mold grow in *Jar A*? _____

3. Did mold grow in *Jar B*? _____

4. Did more mold grow in *Jar B* than in *Jar A*? _____

Draw Your Conclusions:

5. Does moisture cause mold to grow? _____

_____

George Washington Carver

Write an essay on the contributions and life of Dr. George Washington Carver. Do some research. Why do you think Dr. Carver liked agricultural science? Take notes from research sources on a separate sheet of paper, then list and organize your ideas. Choose a title carefully to tell the reader your opinion of Dr. Carver. Remember to edit your essay after writing, and check for spelling, grammar, complete sentences, and style.

_____

_____

_____

_____

_____

_____

_____

_____

_____

_____

_____

_____

_____

_____

_____

_____

_____

_____

_____

_____

_____

George Washington Carver

Match the words from the list below with their correct meanings. Write each word on the line by its meaning.

fungi   legumes   hyphae

mycology   agriculturalist   puffball

mold

_____ 1. a large, ball-shaped fungus

_____ 2. a type of fungus

_____ 3. a branch of botany dealing with fungi

_____ 4. a scientist who develops better ways to raise crops and livestock

_____ 5. a family of plants that have seeds growing in pods

_____ 6. a form of life that includes mushrooms, molds, and puffballs

_____ 7. the root-like growths of a fungus

Chapter 3:
CHARLES DREW
(June 3, 1904–1950)
Medical Doctor
Biologist

☆ Dr. Charles Drew was born in 1904 in Washington, D.C.

☆ Dr. Drew was an outstanding athlete. He made All-American mention in college football.

☆ Dr. Drew attended medical school in Canada at McGill University.

☆ Dr. Drew established blood banks in the United States and England.

☆ Dr. Drew was the first African American to be a member of the American Board of Surgery.

☆ Dr. Drew advanced the idea that plasma could be stored for long periods of time and used for blood transfusions.

☆ Dr. Drew died in 1950.

Charles Drew

Many great scientists throughout history have devoted their lives to the study of blood. An African American man who deserves recognition for his outstanding work in blood research is Dr. Charles Drew. Dr. Drew's most important contribution in the area of blood research was the establishment of blood banks. Blood banks are places where blood is stored.

During World War II, many lives were lost because no one knew how to give the soldiers immediate blood transfusions. A blood transfusion is when blood is taken from one person and given to another person who needs it. Dr. Drew analyzed the problem. He came up with a method for providing persons with their own blood types if they were injured. This meant that injured soldiers could get quick transfusions and be saved.

The first problem that Dr. Drew had to solve was to prevent coagulation. When blood types are not compatible, coagulation occurs to a dangerous level, and the blood does not flow properly. Coagulation means that blood clots, or forms small masses of blood clumped together. Dr. Drew realized that if lives were going to be saved through transfusion, there had to be some way to keep the blood flowing instead of coagulating. Coagulation can cause death.

Using whole blood, Dr. Drew knew that the storage time would be short—a week. Whole blood is blood which has not been separated from the cells. Dr. Drew had to come up with a way to preserve blood for a longer period of time.

After long hours of research, Dr. Drew discovered that a life-saving alternative was to give transfusions with plasma, not whole blood. Plasma is the liquid portion of the blood which has been separated from the cells. Plasma can be stored for long periods of time under refrigerated conditions.

BLOOD

Blood is made up of two basic parts—plasma and blood cells. Plasma, which Dr. Drew used in his blood banks, is the liquid part. It is made up of water; plasma proteins such as albumin, fibrinogen, antibodies, and hormones; products of digestion, such as glucose, fatty acids, amino acids, vitamins, and minerals; waste products; and minerals. The plasma carries most of the carbon dioxide from the lungs.

The solid part of the blood is made up of red blood cells, white blood cells and platelets. These cells carry out different functions in keeping your body fit.

Red Blood Cells	White Blood Cell	Platelets

Red blood cells carry oxygen throughout body tissues. After these substances are delivered, the red blood cells pick up some carbon dioxide and wastes so that your body can get rid of them. Blood that has little oxygen is dark blue. Blood that is rich in oxygen is bright red.

Doctors often check to see if a patient's white blood cell count is high. When this happens, a doctor knows that the patient's body is fighting against attack. White blood cells fight foreign substances, like infections, that can cause illness or even death. These cells also clean up the body's dead cells and other debris.

Platelets are cells with outer points that look like spines. When a person bleeds from an injury, the platelets pile up in the wound. They plug the opening to stop the bleeding. This causes a clot to form. Platelets also help the blood vessels to contract, which reduces bleeding.

Red blood cells are disk-shaped. They are very tiny. Scientists think that you may have as many as 25-trillion red blood cells in your body. Red blood cells have no nucleus. Red blood cells are not able to reproduce by themselves. Hemoglobin is the substance that makes red blood cells red. Hemoglobin is the red protein substance in a red blood cell which carries oxygen to cells. White blood cells have a nucleus and are larger than red blood cells. Platelets are the smallest cells in the blood, and are disk-shaped.

BLOOD TYPES

Blood banks are like regular banks where money is kept until needed. Blood is stored in banks until it is needed.

When a patient needs blood, the doctor must first know the patient's blood type. If you were to receive blood that did not match your type, you could die. Clumping occurs when a person does not receive the blood that matches his or her blood type.

The Four Basic Blood Types	
A	B
AB	O Universal

For example, a person with type A blood can only receive type A blood or type O blood. Type O blood is a universal type, and it can be given to everyone with every blood type.

Dr. Charles Drew set up blood banks. He organized blood banks in the United States and in London during World War II.

Charles Drew

> This demonstration should be done by the teacher only. Students should use Hands-On Activity Sheet #2 to answer questions related to the demonstration.

You Will Need:

- human serum - Type A, Type B (can be obtained from biological supply stores)
- microscope
- match
- alcohol
- slide
- cotton
- a clean needle or pin
- black marker
- eyedropper

!!! Safety Caution
Protect yourself by wearing safety goggles, rubber gloves, and a lab apron.

1. With a black marker, draw a line down the middle of the slide.

2. Write AA on one half and AB on the other half. (AA means "Anti A," while AB means "Anti B".)

3. Using the eyedropper, place a drop of the B serum in the space marked AA.

4. In the space marked AB, place a drop of A serum.

5. Clean your little finger with the alcohol and cotton.

6. Using a needle or pin, carefully prick the end of your little finger and squeeze out a drop of blood, catching it on the end of the match.

7. Using the end of the match, place the blood in the Anti A serum.

8. With the other end of the match, mix in a drop of blood with the Anti B serum.

9. After several minutes, have students come up to observe the slide under the microscope.

Charles Drew

1. What is the purpose of the demonstration? _____

   _____

2. List the four basic blood types. _____

   _____

3. What is clotting? _____

   _____

   _____

4. When does clotting occur? _____

   _____

   _____

5. Draw a clotting and non-clotting cell.

   | | | |
   |--------------------| |------------------------|
   | | | |

   Clotting Cell   Non-Clotting Cell

6. What type of blood cells clot? _____

   _____

7. Why is it important for doctors to know a person's blood type? ____

   _____

   _____

8. What is your teacher's blood type? _____

   _____

9. The next time you go to the doctor, try to find out what your
   blood type is.

Charles Drew

You Will Need:

- resource materials/library
- cardboard
- typewriter or word processor if available
- marker
- ring holders
- string

Students will learn about the function and purpose of white blood cells, red blood cells, and platelets through a hands-on activity. To understand better the function and purpose of the various types of blood cells, students should first research the topic.

1. Form small groups of 3–5 students.

2. Give students time to find and use outside resources and information, including the library and information groups or local doctors.

3. Class time will be needed to discuss the assignment. Projects should be completed within 2–3 weeks.

4. Each group's goal is to complete:

    a. A chart of each type of blood, with a short essay describing each.

    b. Each cell should have a creative design, such as a collage.

5. Place the cell charts on white cardboard to display all three cell types, or three charts could be held together by heavy string or ring holders. Charts should be large enough to put on display.

Charles Drew

You Will Need:

- clay
- 2 shoe-box tops
- stapler and staples
- string
- small marble
- cardboard strips
- masking tape
- scissors
- small beads
- glue
- 2-inch (5.08-centimeter) cardboard disks

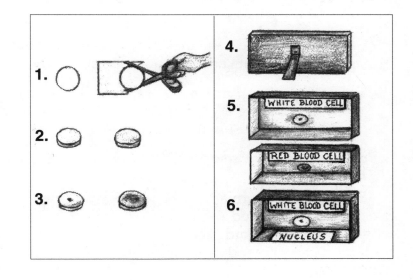

You will learn to distinguish between basic structures of white and red blood cells.

1. Cut out two 2-inch (5.08 centimeters) circular cardboard disks.

2. Cover both cardboard disks with a 1/2-inch – 1-inch thick layer (1.27 – 2.54 centimeters) of clay.

3. Place a small marble in the center of one of the disks. On the other disk, use small beads to form an inner circle one inch (2.54 centimeters) from the outside of the disk. One disk represents a white blood cell. Red blood cells have no nucleus.

4. Staple your cardboard stands 1 1/2 inches (3.81 centimeters) behind each shoe-box top. Glue your disks in each shoe-box top.

5. Using a 2 1/2-inch – 3-inch (6.35 – 7.62 centimeters) strip of masking tape, write the names "white blood cells" and "red blood cells," and put the strips inside the top of the proper shoe-box tops.

6. On a 2-inch (5.08-centimeter) strip of masking tape, write "nucleus" and place it at the bottom of the shoe box that has the white blood cell model.

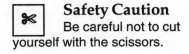

Safety Caution
Be careful not to cut yourself with the scissors.

Charles Drew

Do a research project and make a report on one of the following. You may want to write an essay or create an oral report.

a. Estimate the approximate number of lives Dr. Drew saved by discovering a way of storing plasma in blood banks. Explain your estimate and your logic.

b. Compare Dr. Drew with Paul Robeson in a 2–3 page essay.

c. Interview a Red Cross Blood Bank worker or a hematologist. Share your interview by writing it newspaper style.

_____

_____

_____

_____

_____

_____

_____

_____

_____

_____

_____

_____

_____

_____

_____

Charles Drew

Match the words from the list below with their correct meanings. Write each word on the line by its meaning.

blood bank	blood transfusion	blood type
coagulation	hemoglobin	plasma
platelets	red blood cells	white blood cells
whole blood		

_____ 1. the process of taking blood from one person and giving it to another person who needs it

_____ 2. a blood clot or small mass of blood clumped together

_____ 3. the liquid portion of the blood that is made up of water and dissolved proteins, digested foods, waste products, and minerals

_____ 4. the part of the blood that transports water, oxygen, food, carbon dioxide, and wastes

_____ 5. the part of the blood that fights attack by foreign substances

_____ 6. the smallest part of the blood that causes clotting to help stop bleeding

_____ 7. a place where blood is stored until it is needed

_____ 8. the kind of blood a person has—A, B, AB, or O

_____ 9. the blood that is made up of plasma and blood cells

_____ 10. the substance in red blood cells that carries oxygen to the cells red

Chapter 4:
MEREDITH GOURDINE
(born 1929)
Physicist
Scientist
Engineer

☆ Dr. Gourdine was born in 1929.

☆ Dr. Gourdine graduated from Cornell University. He received his Ph.D. in Engineering Science from California Institute of Technology.

☆ Dr. Gourdine is President of his own company, *Gourdine Systems, Inc.*

☆ Dr. Gourdine was an outstanding athlete in college. He won the Silver Medal in the 1952 Olympics in the broad jump.

☆ Dr. Gourdine's inventions include:

1. the electrogasdynamics channel
2. the high voltage generating equipment
3. the mark I generator
4. an automotive exhaust precipitator
5. a dust monitor

☆ Dr. Gourdine has also done work with plasma cell techniques which would make electrical power cheaper and reduce air pollution.

Meredith Gourdine

Like Dr. Charles Drew, Dr. Meredith Gourdine was an outstanding scientist as well as an outstanding athlete. Meredith Gourdine won the silver medal in the 1952 Olympics in the broad jump. Later, Meredith Gourdine became Dr. Meredith Gourdine, receiving his Ph.D. in engineering science.

One of Dr. Gourdine's major interests is protecting the environment and developing alternate methods for producing energy. Much of the electricity you use is produced by generators powered by water, or hydroelectric power. Unfortunately, in many areas, water supplies are in short supply because of drought, increasing consumption, and other causes. Dr. Gourdine recognized the problem and developed the electrogasdynamics channel, or E.G.D.C. In the E.G.D.C., gas is converted into electricity as it moves through specially designed circular channels.

To understand Dr. Gourdine's E.G.D.C., you must understand the concept of energy. You have energy, and your body has energy. Your body is like a machine that must have a source of energy to keep it going. Food is the only source of energy. By eating healthy meals, you have the energy source for all the mental and physical tasks you want to perform. Energy is the force that enables something to do work.

Energy Source	Type Of Work That Results
1. Coal	Heats factories, homes
2. Water Falling	Makes electricity
3. Gasoline	Makes planes fly, cars go
4. Dynamite	Blasts away mountains, buildings
5. Wind	Makes windmills turn

There are two types of energy: potential and kinetic. Potential energy is stored energy, just as food may be stored and used at a later time. For example, an archer has *stored energy* in his or her body. When the archer pulls the arrow against the bow string, stored energy is transferred to the bow. Now the bow has stored energy. Once the bow is released and the arrow is shot, the potential energy of the bow becomes the arrow's kinetic energy. Kinetic energy is the energy of motion.

The conversion of flowing gas into electricity is an important source of energy today. Other types of energy which are important include *chemical* energy which can be found, for example, in coal that gives off heat energy when burned. *Mechanical energy* is another type. It is produced by machines. The pistons of a motor give the engine the power to move a car.

Electricity

When you turn on a light switch in a room, energy is set into motion. Electrons are set in motion on a set of wires providing the electrical energy needed to light the bulb in the room. Electrons are negatively charged particles that revolve around the nucleus of an atom. Once electrons are set in motion over a wire, a flow of electricity is started. A current of electricity is produced.

For the home, the power source used to set the electrons into motion is large turbines. The turbines turn generators which move electromagnets. The electromagnets cause the electrons to move. When you turn on a light switch, the energy lights your home.

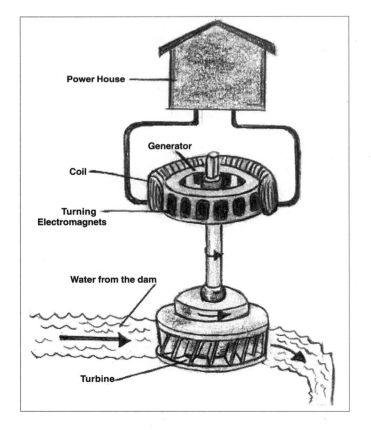

Power House

Generator

Coil

Turning
Electromagnets

Water from the dam

Turbine

Turbines, generators, electromagnets, and wires provide the electricity needed in homes.

Static Electricity

Before Dr. Gourdine's work, there were other scientists who laid the foundation. One scientist was William Gilbert. Gilbert discovered the most basic type of electrical energy, static electricity. Static electricity is electricity which is "still" or stationary, not moving or flowing.

The circles with the minus signs represent the negatively-charged particles of the atom called electrons. They circle the nucleus which is made up of protons and neutrons. Protons have a positive charge (+). Neutrons have no charge, so the nucleus is positive. In an atom, there are as many negatively charged particles as positively charged particles, so the atom is electrically neutral.

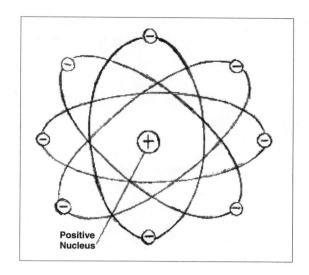

Atom

The electrons in some objects can be transferred. When this happens, the object has fewer electrons. Then the object has fewer negative charges than positive charges. For example, if a plastic comb is rubbed with a piece of wool or fur, the comb becomes negatively charged because of the electrons received from the cloth. When a negatively charged object is placed close to a neutral object (like paper) the neutral object is attracted to the negatively charged object. This is an example of static electricity.

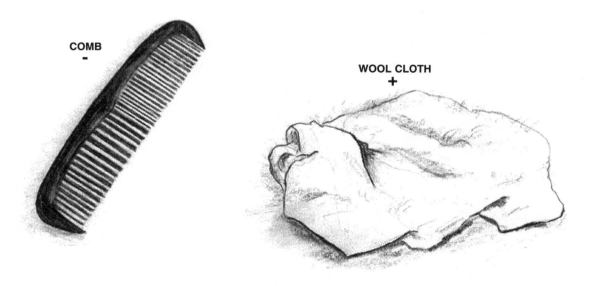

When a comb is rubbed with a wool cloth, it becomes negatively charged, producing static electricity.

Thanks to Dr. Gourdine, the E.G.D.C. produces power. Electrogasdynamics channels are also used to apply protective coatings, as shown in the diagram below.

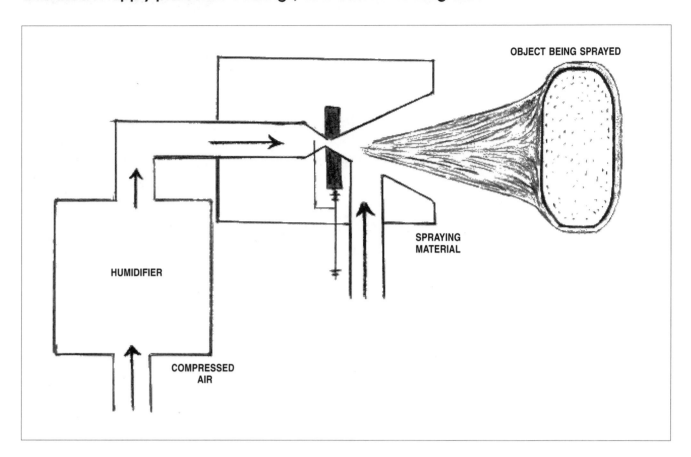

OBJECT BEING SPRAYED

SPRAYING
MATERIAL

HUMIDIFIER

COMPRESSED
AIR

Meredith Gourdine

You Will Need:

- a pencil
- paper, torn into small pieces (about 0.3937 inch or 1 centimeter square)
- a small piece of wool cloth

Note: This experiment works best when it is not damp or rainy.

Static electricity is still electricity, or electricity that is not flowing. It is the opposite of flowing electricity, such as the electricity you use to turn on the lights in your room. When you turn on the light switch, you make the electricity flow over wires to the lights.

The electrons in an atom are negatively charged, but they can be transferred to another object to change its charge. But what happens when objects that have the same electrical charges come together? The objects will either attract each other, or they will repel each other. Do you know which? You can perform an experiment to find out.

First, you must formulate your hypothesis. Do like charges attract each other? Do they repel each other? Write your hypothesis below.

1. _____

_____

_____

Now, experiment to test your hypothesis. Record your results on the chart.

A. The paper is neutral. It has the same number of negative and positive charges. Tear it into small pieces, about one square centimeter (0.3937 inch) each or smaller.

B. You can use friction to change the charge of the pencil. Rubbing the wool on the pencil makes negative electrons move from the wool to the pencil. The pencil becomes negatively charged.

C. What happened? Write your results on the chart on page 34.

Object	Charge	Results
paper	neutral	none
pencil	positive	none
pencil rubbed with wool		
pencil rubbed with wool when placed near paper		

Was your hypothesis correct?

On the basis of your experiment, write a law about like charges on the lines below.

2. _____

_____

_____

_____

Meredith Gourdine

You Will Need:

- a 1.5 volt dry cell or flashlight battery
- 2 insulated copper wires, 20–22 gauge, each about 9.8425 inches (25 centimeters) long
- a small light socket with a flashlight bulb in it
- a small screwdriver for use on the light socket
- wire strippers, or wire cutters
- plastic household tape or electrical tape

Safety Caution
You may wish to wear rubber gloves in order to protect against shocking yourself while completing this experiment.

When you turn on a light switch, you put energy into motion. You make electricity flow along a wire to your lights. To do this, you use an electrical circuit, or circle of wires for the electrons to move along. If the circuit is closed, all the wires are touching and the electrons can flow. If the circuit is open, it is broken and incomplete, and the electrons cannot flow.

You can test what happens when a circuit is closed and what happens when it is open.

1. First, remove 1–2 centimeters (0.3937–0.7874 inches) of the insulation off the ends of both pieces of wire.

2. Connect the bare end of one wire to the positive (+) terminal of the battery. Then connect the bare end of the other wire to the negative (-) terminal of the battery. **Note:** The circuit is now open and incomplete.

3. Screw the light bulb into the socket.

4. Unscrew the screws on the socket base a little. Bend the bare ends of the wires so they fit around the screws.

5. Now close the circuit. Screw the screws down with the screwdriver to hold the other ends of the wires securely on the socket base.

Note Depending on your battery, the terminals may both be on top of the battery, or one may be on the bottom. They should be labeled as + and -. Also, you may have to tape your wire onto the terminals if there are no connectors.

1. The circuit is closed. What happened? _____

_____

_____

2. Disconnect one wire. The circuit is now open. What happened? _____

_____

_____

Meredith Gourdine

You Will Need:

- a dictionary
- a typewriter or word processor
- OPTIONAL: a camera, film, and funds to pay for developing the film*
- reference materials on Dr. Gourdine
- cardboard
- glue

You may wish to complete this activity as a class, in small groups, or individually.

1. Students may wish to write to Cornell University (Ithaca, NY 14853) for pictures and biographical information about Dr. Gourdine. Dr. Gourdine graduated from Cornell. Or you may use copies of reference sources about Dr. Gourdine.

2. If possible, photograph various types of equipment that are a part of an electrical power plant, e.g. turbines. Develop the film.

3. Complete a photo essay about Dr. Gourdine and his work.

4. Display your photo essay.

_____

_____

_____

_____

_____

_____

_____

_____

_____

* OPTIONAL: If funds for film development are not available for the class, this step may be omitted and magazine photos used instead.

Meredith Gourdine

Match the words from the list below with their correct meanings. Write each word on the line by its meaning.

atom   electron   chemical energy

static electricity   hydroelectric power   kinetic energy

mechanical energy   potential energy   proton

electrogasdynamics channel   neutron

_____ 1. the electricity that is produced by generators powered by water

_____ 2. a specially designed channel in which electrical energy is produced by the flow of gas

_____ 3. stored energy

_____ 4. energy that is expressed as motion

_____ 5. energy that can be found, such as the heat energy given off when coal is burned

_____ 6. energy produced by machines, such as the pistons of a car

_____ 7. the negative particle that circles the nucleus of an atom

_____ 8. the smallest part of an element with the properties of the element

_____ 9. the charges of electricity produced by friction; it is still, not moving or flowing

_____ 10. the positive particle that is part of the nucleus of an atom

_____ 11. the particle that is part of the nucleus of an atom and that has no charge

Chapter 5:
ERNEST JUST
(August 14, 1883–October 27, 1946)
Biologist
Scientist

☆ Dr. Just was born in Charleston, South Carolina in 1883.

☆ Dr. Just was educated at Kimball Academy, Dartmouth College, and the University of Chicago. He graduated from Dartmouth with honors.

☆ Dr. Just was the first person to receive the National Association for the Advancement of Colored People's (NAACP) Spingarn Medal for his work in improving medical education at African American universities.

☆ Dr. Just did research on cells, making advances in learning about cell function, particularly in single- and multi-celled animals.

☆ Dr. Just published two books.

☆ Dr. Just died on October 27, 1946, at the age of 58.

Ernest Just

In the field of biology and biological research, Dr. Ernest Just is a man of color who stands out. Dr. Just is recognized as an authority on the structure of the cell. And understanding the cell is a key step in understanding life.

For many years, scientists thought that the cell nucleus was the most important part of the cell. They were wrong. Dr. Just discovered through his research that the cell's cytoplasm was as important as the nucleus. This discovery was contrary to the beliefs held by biologists in the 1930s. As a result of Just's discovery, scientists began to take a closer look at the interworkings of the many parts of the animal cell.

More About Cells

Scientists such as Dr. Just have studied the structure and function of cells for years. Scientists study cells to learn about the smallest unit of all living things. Anything that does not have cells is not a living thing. What are some things that do not have cells? Only nonliving things lack cells.

Imagine watching the Superbowl football championship. What do you think makes a football team good enough to win a Superbowl championship? Is it the tackles? the backs? No—a team becomes a Superbowl champ because all the tackles, guards, running backs, and other players work together to do the job. The running backs could not score if there were no guards or tackles to block for them.

Dr. Just saw that the structure of cells was a team effort, interconnected, like a Superbowl championship football team. He didn't accept the belief at the time that the nucleus, a small rounded bead-like part of the cell, completed all the functions of the cell. He found, instead, that the nucleus did not do everything, but it controlled all the workings of the cell. The *cytoplasm*, the part of the cell outside of the nucleus, and the *ectoplasm*, the dense outer part of the cytoplasm, were practically ignored by biologists before Dr. Just. But after many years of research, Dr. Just found that the cell depended on the ectoplasm, as it did the nucleus and cytoplasm, for the complete development of the individual cell.

Ten Great African American Men of Science **39**

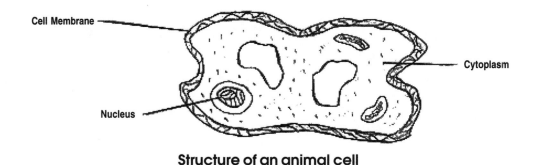

Cell Membrane

Cytoplasm

Nucleus

Structure of an animal cell

Body Cells

The cells in the body also function as a team, just as football players do. The body functions just like an organization. There are different types of cells in the body, each with its own unique responsibilities.

A group of cells that functions to do one specialized job is called tissue. In your body, there are groups of bone cells forming bone tissue, muscle cells forming muscle tissue, nerve cells forming nerve tissue, and blood cells forming blood tissue.

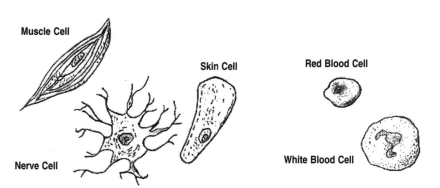

Muscle Cell

Skin Cell

Red Blood Cell

Nerve Cell

White Blood Cell

Tissue cells form skin, muscles, nerves, and blood cells.

By discovering more about the inner workings of the cell, Dr. Just helped science come closer to understanding how the smallest unit of life works. To make any progress in understanding how the entire body works, you must understand the cellular level.

Ernest Just

You Will Need:

- plastic jar with secure, safe top
- access to a pond or puddle of water
- hard-boiled egg yolk
- microscope and slide
- eyedropper

Much of Dr. Just's research centered around marine life. He studied several members of the genus *nereis*. They are commonly called *clam worms*. You can do some marine investigation of your own. Your ocean can be a small pond, or a puddle of rain water.

1. Go to the pond or puddle and fill the jar half full with water. Cap it securely.

2. Bring your jar to class and place it in a warm place.

3. Add bits of hard boiled egg yolks to the water.

4. Leave the jar for a week, letting the yolk decay.

5. As the yolk decays, bacteria will form, so watch for decay. One-celled organisms sometimes live off bacteria.

6. Each day, record your observations on page 42. After there is yolk decay, examine a drop of the pond water under the microscope. What do you see? Is there any movement? Do you think the movement is made by a water protist, which is a one-celled organism? Why?

_____

_____

_____

_____

_____

_____

_____

_____

HANDS-ON ACTIVITY SHEET # 1: OBSERVING ONE-CELLED ANIMALS
(continued)

Record your observations:

Day 1 _____

_____

_____

_____

Day 2 _____

_____

_____

_____

Day 3 _____

_____

_____

_____

Day 4 _____

_____

_____

_____

Day 5 _____

_____

_____

_____

Ernest Just

You Will Need:

- string
- scissors
- food coloring
- water
- a clear plastic bowl
- a length of sausage casing, available at the butcher's counter in grocery stores
- a stop watch
- various colored liquids, such as brewed coffee or tea, colas, milk, dark syrup, tomato sauce, and others

Safety Caution
Be careful not to cut yourself with the scissors.

Safety Caution
Make sure your students are not allergic to any of these substances before doing this experiment.

Safety Caution
Be sure to protect your clothing during this experiment by wearing an apron.

Dr. Just studied one-celled animals. Cells can pick up or dispose of substances through their cell walls. This process is called osmosis. Use the following experiment to see how osmosis works.

Hypothesis: Liquid and substances can move back and forth through the cell membrane.

1. Cut a short length of the sausage casing. Tie one end tightly closed with a piece of string.

2. Mix food coloring with some water. Fill the sausage casing with this water. Tie the other end tightly closed with a piece of string.

3. Fill the bowl with clear water, and put the sausage casing in it.

4. Use the stop watch to time how long it takes for the colored water to begin seeping through the sausage casing into the clear water. Take notes of your observations.

5. Fill a second sausage casing with clear water and the bowl with colored water. Place the sausage casing in the colored water. See if the colored water seeps into this sausage casing.

Record Your Observations:

1. How long did it take for osmosis to begin transferring colored water from the first sausage casing into the clear water?

_____

2. Did colored water seep into the second sausage casing? _____

   How long did it take for this to happen? _____

HANDS-ON ACTIVITY SHEET # 2: EXPERIMENTING WITH OSMOSIS (continued)

Does osmosis work at the same rate for all substances?

Follow the procedure on page 43 to test how long it takes for different substances to be transferred from sausage casings to clear water in a bowl. Record your findings in the chart below.

Rate of Osmosis

Substance	Did Osmosis Occur?	How Long before Osmosis Began

Record Your Observations:

1. Does osmosis affect various substances differently?

_____

2. Which substance began to transfer most quickly?

_____

3. Did any substances not transfer at all? If so, name them.

_____

Ernest Just

Write or draw your answers in the spaces provided.

1. What was the name of the medal given to Dr. Just in 1915 for his work in improving medical education at African American universities?

   _____

2. What important discovery did Dr. Just make? _____

   _____

   _____

3. How many books did Dr. Just publish? _____

   _____

4. What is a cell? _____

   _____

   _____

5. What is tissue? _____

   _____

   _____

6. Draw a cell.

Match the words from the list below with their correct meanings. Write each word on the line by its meaning.

NAACP   cytoplasm   nucleus

ectoplasm   Spingarn Medal

_____   1. the achievement award given by the NAACP

_____   2. the part of the cell outside of the nucleus

_____   3. the abbreviation for a civil rights organization known as the National Association for the Advancement of Colored People

_____   4. the outer layer of the cytoplasm

_____   5. a small rounded bead-like part of a cell

Chapter 6:
GARRETT A. MORGAN
(March 4, 1877–1963)
Inventor

☆ Garrett A. Morgan was born March 4, 1877.

☆ Garrett A. Morgan had no formal education past the elementary level.

☆ His first invention was a hair-straightening cream for African Americans.

☆ Today's gas mask was the result of Mr. Morgan's invention of the safety hood.

☆ He invented the world's first traffic signal system. He sold the rights for this system to the General Electric Corp. for a mere $40,000 in 1923.

☆ He was the founder of the *Cleveland Call and Post,* a weekly African American newspaper published in Cleveland, Ohio.

☆ Garrett A. Morgan died in 1963.

Garrett A. Morgan

Garrett A. Morgan was one of many great African American inventors who helped to make your community safer. During his years in Cleveland, Ohio, he invented two devices which have saved the lives of millions of people—the smoke mask and the traffic signal.

Garrett A. Morgan had the opportunity to prove his inventive genius to the nation when he used one of his inventions to go into a mine following an explosion and saved the lives of trapped miners. That invention was the smoke mask.

Mr. Morgan was motivated to develop another important safety invention when he witnessed an accident between a car and a horse-drawn carriage. You associate the colors red, green, and yellow with the traffic signal. Our traffic signals today are patterned after the first traffic signal invented by Garrett A. Morgan. The traffic signal invented by Mr. Morgan served the same purpose as today's traffic signal. When you think about safety, think about Garrett A. Morgan.

Accident Prevention

Mr. Morgan spent a great deal of time thinking about safety, but he did more than think. He did something to prevent accidents. You do not have to be an inventor like Mr. Morgan to prevent accidents in your home and community. The majority of accidents are caused by human error. By analyzing accidents by location and type, you can develop your own program to prevent accidents.

Location of Accidents

Some common locations where accidents occur are:

- bathrooms
- stairways
- yard areas
- kitchens
- living rooms
- slippery floors
- unlighted areas, and
- garages.

Types of Accidents

Burns can happen in areas with unusually hot water, such as bathtubs, sinks, and laundry facilities. Exposed electrical wires and stoves can cause burns if there is body contact. Burns can be prevented by avoiding contact with hot liquids, hot objects, and fire.

Asphyxiation and Suffocation

Asphyxiation is caused when a person has a high concentration of carbon monoxide in the bloodstream. The person is poisoned by the carbon monoxide, and stops breathing. Carbon monoxide is a poisonous gas that is odorless. It comes from gas pipes that leak, furnaces, and the exhaust from automobiles, trucks, and various other machines that burn fuels which contain carbons, but only when proper ventilation is not present. To avoid asphyxiation, you should:

1. Never run an engine without having proper ventilation.

2. All gas fixtures, such as furnaces, stoves, and any pipes that carry a gas fuel should be inspected for leaks regularly by a qualified person.

Suffocation

Suffocation is caused when the oxygen supply is prevented from reaching the lungs. If you were underwater and unable to hold your breath any longer, your lungs would fill with water when you tried to breathe. Your oxygen supply would be cut off. You would suffocate.

Injury and Death by Gunshot

Guns are not toys and are very dangerous. If guns are kept in your house, they should be locked away. You should never handle guns with any ammunition in them. Any gun could give you a horrible surprise. It could be loaded and, if discharged even in play, could cause serious injury or death to you, a friend, or a loved one.

Poisoning

Apathy and negligence can cause poisoning deaths. Small children and pets are very curious. Unless care is taken to lock cabinets and doors, poisons that are left within reach can be harmful or even fatal. Sometimes even adults mistake a bottle of poison for medicine and take it. Accidents by poisoning can be prevented by:

1. keeping poisons out of the reach of children and pets.

2. reading labels to check for poisons before you open a bottle, a jar, or package.

3. putting proper labels on medicines and poisons.

4. placing safety caps on bottles and jars so children cannot open them easily.

5. educating young brothers and sisters about the dangers of poisons and how to recognize bottles that might contain poisons.

Where Accidents Occur

A large amount of your time is spent in your home, so it is important to know where accidents are most likely to occur. And it is important to know some preventative measures you can take to make your home safer. Look at the chart below. Where does the highest percentage of fatal accidents occur in the home?

Fatal Home Accidents

Location	Percentage
Dining Room	3.4%
Living Room	5.9%
Bedroom	25.6%
Bathroom	3.5%
Kitchen	10.3%
Outside Stairs	3.9%
Basement	1.7%
Inside Stairs	7.4%
Porch	3.3%
Yard	11.6%
Garage	1.1%

Safety Organizations

Safety organizations, national conferences, and legislation have brought improvements in safety education. For example, it was at the Second International Exposition of Safety and Sanitation in New York City that Garrett A. Morgan received a gold medal as first prize for his invention of the safety hood. The safety hood led to the invention of the gas mask. During the Gulf War, you saw how important devices similar to the gas mask are.

One of the best-known safety organizations in the U.S. is the American Automobile Association. Many efforts of the A.A.A. have been devoted to traffic safety in schools. The association helped to organize Safety Patrols and Driver's Education classes.

The Association of Casualty and Surety Companies has been in existence for a long time. This organization has been a pioneer in improving Driver Education Programs for both private and public schools.

Garrett A. Morgan's inventive genius did much to make our lives safer. The traffic signal, which led to our modern traffic lights, has saved millions of lives. Morgan's creativity has helped us all.

Garrett A. Morgan

1. First, do library research to get information about first aid.

2. Next, fill in a prevention and a treatment for each problem below.

3. Then, in small groups, develop a role-play or skit to show safety measures for at least one problem.

SAFETY FIRST

Problem	Prevention	Treatment
Small Cut on Finger	_____	_____
	_____	_____
	_____	_____
Swallowing Poison	_____	_____
	_____	_____
	_____	_____
Fainting	_____	_____
	_____	_____
	_____	_____
Going into Shock	_____	_____
	_____	_____
	_____	_____
Breaking a Bone	_____	_____
	_____	_____
	_____	_____

Garrett A. Morgan

Review the chart on page 50 showing where fatal home accidents occur most often. Make a colorful bar graph of where they occur.

1. First, put the data in order—either increasing or decreasing.

2. Next, select your colors and draw your chart in pencil below.

3. Finally, color-code your bar graph to use colors to represent the five most fatal areas.

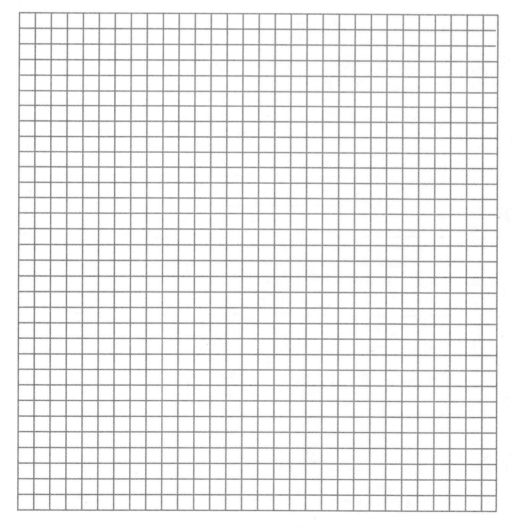

4. Now, review your graph and, for each area, write one suggested prevention technique beside the bar.

Garrett A. Morgan

Write your answers in the spaces provided.

1. Do you think $40,000 was a fair amount of money to receive for an invention that has saved the lives of millions? Explain.

   _____

   _____

2. Do you think Mr. Morgan's inventions of the safety hood and the traffic signal were only beneficial for African American people? Explain.

   _____

   _____

3. What are some things you can do in your home to prevent accidents from happening? List at least five things.

   _____

   _____

   _____

   _____

   _____

4. What can be done to prevent accidents caused by asphyxiation and suffocation? Give at least one answer for each.

   _____

   _____

5. Why are poisons dangerous? _____

   _____

   Why should they be kept out of reach of small children and pets?

   _____

   _____

Chapter 7:
ALVIN POUSSAINT
(born May 15, 1934)
Psychiatrist
Doctor

☆ Dr. Poussaint attended high school in New York.

☆ Dr. Poussaint wrote a book entitled *Why Blacks Kill Blacks*.

☆ Dr. Poussaint is currently Associate Professor of Psychiatry at Harvard Medical School.

Alvin Poussaint

Many people are deeply concerned by the increased use of drugs by African American people. One African American leader who is studying this important issue is Dr. Alvin Poussaint. Dr. Poussaint is an African American man who is a leading authority on analyzing the cause and effect pattern of behavior in the African American community.

From his research, Dr. Poussaint concluded that environmental influences have a great role in determining the response patterns of African American youth. Dr. Poussaint feels that movies that glorify drug dealers and drug use influence the behavioral patterns of urban youth in a negative way. A good example of this kind of behavior was obvious following the release of a movie called *Superfly* in the early 70s which glorified a drug pusher. Young people began to copy some of the movie character's behavioral patterns. They began to wear the same superfly styles portrayed in the movie. Other movies that glorify the martial arts influenced a large number of young people to use karate, but, unfortunately, without understanding or learning the necessary discipline and skills needed to practice this ancient art of self-defense.

Behavior

In analyzing behavior, it is important to understand two basic types of behavior: learned and unlearned. Learned behavior involves training. Unlearned behavior involves no learning; and you just do it naturally, such as sleeping or sneezing.

Many behavioral patterns are learned through environmental influences, or from things in the world around you. Drugs and movies are a part of the environment. Like other things in your environment, they can cause you to make a response. When anything causes a response or reaction, it is called a stimulus. If you were hit on the hand with a stick, what would your response be to this stimulus?

Interpreting a Stimulus

There are five basic senses that tell you when you are experiencing a stimulus. These are the senses of sight, hearing, touch, taste, and smell. Your eyes, ears, and nose enable you to see, hear, and smell. Your tongue and special parts of your mouth help you taste the foods you eat. Nerve endings beneath your skin help you determine how different things feel.

When you see a light or go to the movies, you use your sensory organs to interpret what you hear and see. Two of your sensory organs are your eyes and ears. Impulses go from your sensory organs to the brain, where you interpret them. People use these interpretations to learn about their environments.

Behavior on Television

Dr. Poussaint, in much of his work, feels there are too many programs on television that portray African Americans in a negative manner. He thinks that too many shows present African Americans as comics, rather than as persons in professional roles, such as doctors, lawyers, and teachers.

Because of the issues raised in Dr. Poussaint's work, there are more television programs and movies today than ever before that portray African Americans in a positive manner. But is the presentation fair enough? You will have to decide. Dr. Poussaint's research and work have helped to improve the media to where we are now.

▓▓▓▓▓▓▓▓▓▓▓▓▓▓▓▓▓▓▓▓▓▓▓▓▓▓▓▓▓▓▓▓▓▓▓▓

Alvin Poussaint

Read the behaviors listed in the middle column of the chart.
Write the behaviors under the correct headings.

Learned Behavior		Unlearned Behavior
	Playing Basketball	
	Writing Stories	
	Laughing	
	Counting	
	Swimming	
	Playing Football	
	Snoring	
	Crying	
	Talking	
	Sleeping	
	Sewing	
	Walking	
	Reading	
	Dancing	
	Breathing	
	Running	
	Moving	

Alvin Poussaint

You Will Need:

- at least 25 small objects with edges that are not sharp or unsafe
- a stopwatch or a watch with a second hand

1. Hide the objects so the students cannot see them.

2. Blindfold two students.

3. Place a few (2–5) of the objects within the two students' reach.

4. Have another student time them as they spend 25 seconds touching and feeling the objects without anyone speaking.

5. After 25 seconds, remove the blindfolds and place all 25 objects in the reach of the students.

6. Give each student a piece of paper and have the students write down the objects that they think were in front of them.

Conclusions:

Write your conclusions about the sense of touch.

_____

_____

_____

_____

_____

_____

_____

_____

_____

_____

Alvin Poussaint

Dr. Alvin Poussaint was an advisor to Dr. Bill Cosby on *The Cosby Show* while it was on television. As a psychiatrist, Dr. Poussaint was asked to help decide how to present African Americans in a positive manner on television. Do you think that African Americans are presented fairly and as positively as other people on television? This activity will help you form an opinion.

1. As a class or in small groups, select several television shows that feature African Americans in the main or major roles. Each person or small group should choose a different show.

2. Get your parent(s) or caregiver's permission to watch the show you have selected.

3. As you watch the show, record your responses to it and analysis of it on the top chart on page 61.

4. Now, watch a television show in which non-African Americans are the main characters. Answer the same questions for the second show. Record your responses on the bottom chart on page 61.

5. As a class or in small groups, total the responses and discuss the results. Use these questions to reach your conclusions.

6. Are most of the shows about African Americans comedies? serious dramas? what?

   _____

7. Do most of the shows with African Americans include violence?

   _____

8. Do most of the shows featuring non-African Americans have less violence? less comedy?

   _____

9. From your class or group data, do you conclude that there is a bias on television in the presentation of African Americans? Explain your answer.

   _____

   _____

   _____

Program with African American Major Characters

Name of show: _____

What type of show was it? (Circle one or fill in the blank.)

       crime   comedy   serious drama

  other: _____

Number of African Americans in leading roles: _____

Number of African Americans in minor or insignificant roles: _____

Number of African Americans in positive roles: _____ in negative roles: _____

Conclusions:

_____

_____

_____

Program with Non-African American Major Characters

Name of show: _____

What type of show was it? (Circle one or fill in the blank.)

       crime   comedy   serious drama

  other: _____

Number of African Americans in leading roles: _____

Number of African Americans in minor or insignificant roles: _____

Number of African Americans in positive roles: _____ in negative roles: _____

Conclusions:

_____

_____

_____

Alvin Poussaint

Write your answers in the spaces provided.

1. Name five things in your external environment that you think are good influences. Explain why.

   _____

   _____

   _____

2. Name five things in your environment that you think are bad influences. Explain why.

   _____

   _____

   _____

3. Name the five basic senses. _____

   _____

   _____

4. Name the primary sense organ that is associated with each of the five senses.

   _____

   _____

   _____

5. Could your sense organs function without the brain? Explain. _____

   _____

   _____

   _____

6. What is a stimulus? _____

   _____

   _____

   _____

7. What is a response? _____

_____

_____

8. List five behaviors that are learned responses.

   a. _____

   b. _____

   c. _____

   d. _____

   e. _____

9. List a stimulus for each learned behavior in number 8.

_____

_____

_____

_____

_____

10. List at least two behavioral actions you can take to improve
    yourself.

_____

_____

_____

_____

11. What is a learned behavior? _____

_____

_____

Give an example of:

learned behavior _____

unlearned behavior _____

Chapter 8:
NORBERT RILLIEUX
(March 17, 1806–October 8, 1894)
Engineer
Inventor

☆ Norbert Rillieux was born in 1806.

☆ His father was a wealthy French plantation owner, slave owner, and engineer.

☆ Mr. Rillieux's father invented a cotton-bailing press that was operated by steam.

☆ Mr. Rillieux attended school in Paris.

☆ Mr. Rillieux invented the following things which revolutionized the sugar industry.

- Vacuum-pan evaporator

- Catchall

- Sight glass or lunette

☆ Mr. Rillieux's accomplishments were recognized in such countries as Holland and England, as well as the United States.

☆ Mr. Rillieux developed a draining process of eliminating mosquitoes from swamps.

☆ Mr. Rillieux died in 1894.

Norbert Rillieux

We all enjoy sweet candy, cookies, cakes, and various other products made out of sugar. Too much sugar, like many other food substances, can cause damage to your teeth and health. But your body needs some sugar for energy.

An African American man, Mr. Norbert Rillieux, developed a process that made sugar easy to refine and use. Mr. Rillieux developed a way to process sugar efficiently.

Sugar has been called the foundation of life. Sugar is like gasoline in cars. Gas is the fuel that makes a car run. In our bodies, various forms of sugar provide the energy and heat to keep our bodies going.

When you think of sugar, you may think of white processed crystals. Actually, sugar is not always like this. Before the processed or granulated sugar reaches your table, it is in an unprocessed state and is difficult to use. The man who developed a processing procedure to make sugar more usable was Mr. Norbert Rillieux. Mr. Rillieux was a genius who developed a vacuum pan evaporator. His efficient vacuum pan replaced the old, hard-to-use *Jamaican train* method of processing sugar.

Mr. Rillieux understood that the most important property of sugar was its sweetness.

Atoms

An atom is the smallest part of an element that contains all its properties. Two or more atoms can combine to form a molecule. The molecule is a new substance. Sugar is a combination of carbon, hydrogen, and oxygen atoms.

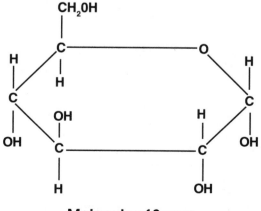

Molecule of Sugar

Sugar Cane Processing

One of the early methods of processing sugar cane was called the Jamaica train. This was a process used on sugar cane plantations. Enslaved people would pour hot sugar cane juice from one kettle into another kettle. This was slow and difficult. This primitive method of sugar processing was a childhood memory that motivated Mr. Rillieux to develop his much improved method for sugar processing, the vacuum pan method.

Modern Sugar Processing

First, sugar cane is brought to the mill in trucks. Then the sugar cane is cleaned. Next, the cleaned sugar cane goes through a shredding mill, and then through pressure rollers. Fourth, sweet juice is squeezed from the sugar cane as it is squeezed through the rollers. Fifth, the sugar cane juice is warmed in large heaters. Sixth, evaporator tanks keep the sugar from scorching. Dr. Rillieux developed this part of the process in the middle 1800s. Seventh, syrup passes from the evaporator tanks to vacuum pans where the excess water is removed from the syrup. Finally in the vacuum pans, the syrup is cooled to the point where crystals form. Crystals of raw sugar are separated from the syrup inside centrifuges.

Sugar Processing

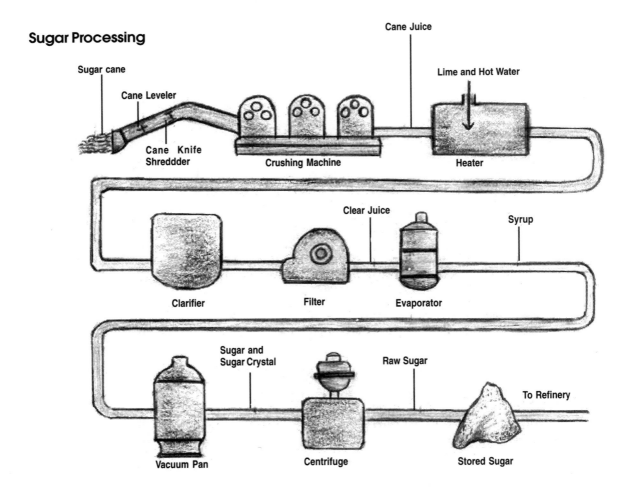

Norbert Rillieux

Do research in your school or neighborhood library to complete the following chart:

Find out the yearly sugar output for each country and state for the same year. Use the same year for the entire chart.

Country	Tons	Year	State	Tons	Year
Nigeria			Florida		
China			Oregon		
Cuba			Alabama		
Mexico			Montana		
India			Texas		
Bahamas			Louisiana		
Australia			Hawaii		
United States			Washington		
France			South Dakota		
Germany			Idaho		
Argentina			California		

My Conclusions:

_____   1. What country has the largest output of sugar in the year you selected?

_____   2. What state has the largest output of sugar in the year you selected?

Norbert Rillieux

You Will Need:

- water
- 10 glasses
- a spoon for each student
- sugar
- salt
- ice cream
- pepper
- vinegar
- baking soda
- flour
- lemon juice
- vanilla flavoring
- 10 small pieces of paper as labels
- pencil or pen

Safety Caution
Make sure you are not allergic to any of these substances before doing this experiment.

Safety Caution
Tasting as a way of identifying substances is safe only when testing foods. It is too dangerous a technique to use for identification of other types of substances.

The sense of taste can help you tell that sugar is dissolved in a cup of water even though you can't see the sugar.

1. Fill the 10 glasses with water.

2. Ask a volunteer to use the spoon to make nine different mixtures of water and the foods listed above. Leave one glass filled with plain water.

3. Write the names of the mixtures on the 10 pieces of paper. Place each paper face down in front of the appropriate glass.

4. Point out that some glasses have clear mixtures and some have cloudy mixtures.

5. Have the students take turns tasting the mixtures.

6. Ask the students to describe what they taste using such words as "salty," "sweet," and "bitter."

7. Conduct a class vote to help the students decide what each mixture contains.

8. Turn over the papers to see how well the students identified each mixture.

My Conclusions:

Use the information you obtained in the activity on page 68 to complete the following chart of foods. The first one has been done for you.

Substance	Property
1. Sugar	Sweet
2. Salt	
3. Water	
4. Ice cream	
5. Pepper	
6. Vinegar	
7. Baking soda	
8. Flour	
9. Lemon juice	
10. Vanilla flavoring	

Norbert Rillieux

Answer the following questions with at least one sentence.

1. Why is sugar so important for the body? _____
_____
_____

2. What is a property of sugar? _____
_____
_____

3. Explain the *Jamaican train process.* _____
_____
_____

4. Why do you think Mr. Rillieux's invention was so important? _____
_____
_____

5. What is a molecule? Are molecules related to sugar? Explain. _____
_____
_____

6. Explain how cane sugar is made. _____
_____
_____

7. Why do you think California produces more sugar than
Wisconsin?
_____
_____

Chapter 9:
DANIEL HALE WILLIAMS
(1856–1931)
Physician
Biologist
Surgeon

☆ Dr. Williams was born in 1856.

☆ Dr. Williams was the first surgeon to successfully open the chest cavity and make repairs to the heart.

☆ Dr. Williams was one of the few physicians during his time period to use Lister's principles of antiseptic surgery.

☆ Dr. Williams was the founder of Provident Hospital. Dr. Williams' Provident Hospital was the first school which prepared African American women to enter the field of nursing.

☆ Dr. Williams' Provident Hospital was the first integrated hospital in the United States.

☆ Dr. Williams served on the staff of some of Chicago's largest hospitals.

☆ Dr. Williams did a great deal to open up the medical field for African American people.

☆ Dr. Williams died in 1931.

Daniel Hale Williams

Dr. Daniel Hale Williams was one of the first African American surgeons of the late 1800s. Because of the social conditions against African Americans of this time, Dr. Williams had to start out doing surgery in backrooms and kitchens. In spite of these poor conditions, Dr. Williams continued practicing many revolutionary advanced procedures. For example, antiseptics were not being used by doctors then, but Dr. Williams used them. Antiseptics are chemicals used to kill germs.

Dr. Williams was not only a pioneer in developing new surgical techniques, he was also a pioneer in establishing quality health facilities for African American people. During the late 1800s, African Americans were treated in charity wards rather than hospitals. This bothered Dr. Williams. So in 1891, Dr. Williams, along with a number of other concerned persons, established the first interracial hospital in the United States. The hospital was called Provident Hospital and Training School Association.

Not only did Provident Hospital open the doors for medical treatment for African Americans, but it also opened the door for the training of African American nurses and interns. This was the first organized school for the training of African American nurses.

During the mid-1960s, a great deal of attention was given to Dr. Christiaan Barnard's successful heart transplant. Prior to this great achievement, little attention was given to operations or transplants related to the heart. But before heart transplants, Dr. Daniel Hale Williams performed the first successful open heart operation. Dr. Williams sewed up the heart of a man who had been stabbed in the heart.

The Human Heart

To understand Dr. Williams' miracle operation, you must understand the heart. The heart is a muscle, about the size of your fist. It has tube-like structures extending from the sides. These tube-like structures are blood vessels called arteries, veins, and capillaries. Arteries are the larger blood vessels. The arteries carry the blood *away* from the heart. Veins are the smaller blood vessels. Veins carry the blood *to* the heart. Capillaries are tiny, and connect the arteries and veins.

Blood flows into the heart through the veins. Blood flows out through the arteries. Any damage to the veins or arteries—for example a bullet or knife wound—can easily cause a person to bleed to death.

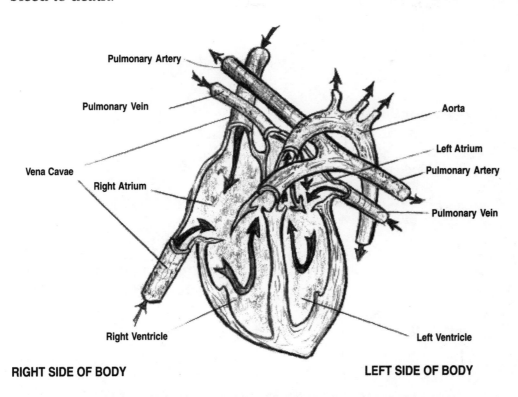

Pulmonary Artery

Pulmonary Vein

Vena Cavae

Right Atrium

Aorta

Left Atrium

Pulmonary Artery

Pulmonary Vein

Right Ventricle

Left Ventricle

RIGHT SIDE OF BODY

LEFT SIDE OF BODY

Blood enters the chambers of the heart through the veins and exits through the arteries.

Dr. Daniel Hale Williams' Miracle Surgery

Mr. James Cornish was in a fight and was stabbed in his heart with a knife. Mr. Cornish was taken to Providence Hospital, where Dr. Williams was on staff. Because of Dr. Williams' advanced techniques, he was able to do surgery. Dr. Williams cut open Mr. Cornish's chest cavity and sewed up his heart. This was the first open heart surgery that was successful. Mr. James Cornish not only survived the operation, he lived for another fifty years! Surely Mr. Cornish would agree that Dr. Williams' operation was miracle surgery!

Daniel Hale Williams

You Will Need:

- stop watch or clock with a second hand

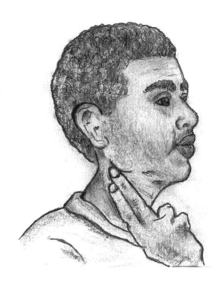

You can take your pulse rate by placing the tips of two fingers on the palm side of your wrist. To obtain a good pulse reading, you must press hard enough to feel your radial artery. Once you feel the pulse beating, hold your fingers on this artery for one minute and count each beat.

1. Take your pulse:

   - While walking

   - After doing 10 push-ups

   - After running in place for 3 minutes

   - After resting quietly for 10 minutes

2. Record your results in the chart below.

!!! Safety Caution
If you have any health problems, discuss them with your teacher before attempting these activities.

Activity	Females' B.P.M.	Males' B.P.M.	Difference
Walking			
Push-ups			
Running in place			
Resting quietly			

*B.P.M. (Beats Per Minute)

My Conclusions:

1. Do different activities affect the pulse rate? _____

   How? _____

2. Was your pulse rate higher or lower during strenuous activity? _____

3. Were average B.P.M.s for the males different from females? _____

   How? _____

Daniel Hale Williams

You Will Need:

• a stethoscope

Using a stethoscope, have students compare the number of heart beats during inactivity (sitting) with the during semi-strenuous activity (running in place). Then answer the following questions:

1. Does the rate of B.P.M. increase during strenuous activity? _____

_____

_____

2. Are the B.P.M.s of girls higher than boys? _____

_____

_____

3. If a person has a total of 240 B.P.M., for three one-minute readings, what would be his or her average B.P.M.?

_____

_____

_____

Daniel Hale Williams

1. Label the basic parts of the heart. You may need to do research.

2. Diagram the flow of blood through the heart.

The Heart

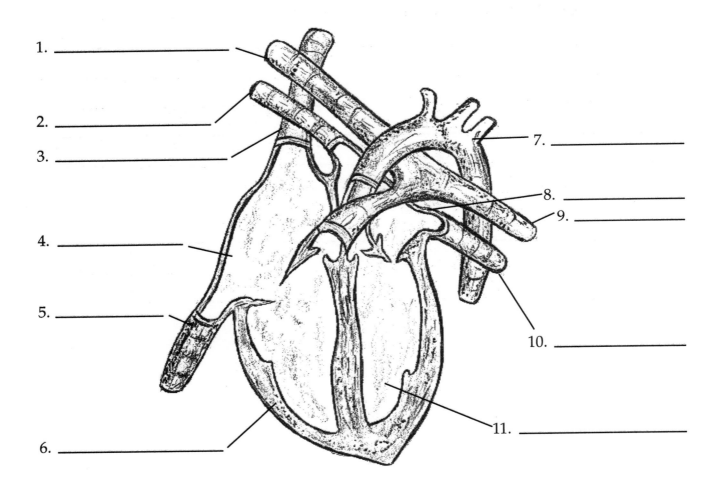

1. _____

2. _____

3. _____

4. _____

5. _____

6. _____

7. _____

8. _____

9. _____

10. _____

11. _____

Daniel Hale Williams

Write your answers in the spaces provided.

1. How are veins and arteries different? _____

_____

_____

2. Of the following, which one would be used to measure the pulse rate? Check your answer.

    _____ a. pin

    _____ b. thermometer

    _____ c. stethoscope

    _____ d. fingertips

3. In what year was Dr. Daniel Hale Williams born? Check your answer.

    _____ a. 1804

    _____ b. 1856

    _____ c. 1909

    _____ d. 1920

4. Check the item that was *not* done by Dr. Williams.

    _____ a. insisted on the need for using antiseptics

    _____ b. discovered how blood flows through the body

Chapter 10:
LOUIS TOMPKINS WRIGHT
(1891–1952)
Physician
Scientist
Surgeon

☆ Dr. Wright was born in 1891.

☆ Dr. Wright was the first African American doctor to be appointed to the staff of a New York hospital.

☆ Dr. Wright was the first African American doctor to experiment with antibiotics.

☆ Dr. Wright developed the intradermal method of vaccination for smallpox.

☆ Dr. Wright won the Spingarn Medal in 1940 for his efforts in fighting racial discrimination in and out of the medical profession.

☆ With his daughter, Dr. Jane C. Wright, Dr. Louis Tompkins Wright did extensive work with chemotherapy which is used in the treatment of cancer.

☆ Dr. Wright died in 1952.

▚▚▚▍█▐▚▚▍█▐▚▚▍█▐▚▚▍█▐▚▚▍█▐▚▚▍█▐▚▚▍█

Louis Tompkins Wright

If Dr. Louis Tompkins Wright had been an athlete, he would have pleased his coaches because of his ability to be first. Dr. Wright achieved a number of medical "firsts." He was the first African American to be appointed to a New York hospital. He was the first African American surgeon on the New York Police Department. He was the first African American person to work and experiment with Aureomycin, an antibiotic, on humans. One could easily say that Dr. Wright was the Jesse Owens of the medical profession.

Dr. Wright received much recognition for his efforts in developing a unique method for being vaccinated against smallpox. The method was called the intradermal technique. By using this technique during World War I, he eliminated the many bad side effects that had occurred with the old method.

Do you have a vaccination scar? If you do, the scar indicates that you have probably been protected against smallpox.

Antibodies - A Major Line of Defense

The body has many defenses against diseases. Your skin and its mucus-producing cells are the first line of defense. White blood cells provide internal defenses against foreign bacteria.

Dr. Wright recognized that the body had internal and external defenses. When he developed his theory for a new method of smallpox vaccination, he knew that antibodies were essential in fighting off disease once the skin was broken.

To understand body defenses, compare them with the defensive alignment of a football team.

On a football team, offensive players cannot score unless they penetrate or break through the defensive alignment of the other team. In many cases, you see runners stopped at the line of scrimmage. What usually has happened is that the player has been stopped by a down lineman. The same kind of situation occurs when bacteria enter your body. But, if the bacteria somehow survive the skin, they have to deal with the other body defenses, such as white blood cells and antibodies.

Antibodies at Work

Do you remember getting your vaccination against smallpox? Do you remember how it was done? Perhaps your arm was pricked or scratched. This method is called the *scratch method.* There are many bad side effects, including scarring. Dr. Wright developed the intradermal method which eliminated most undesirable side effects, including scarring.

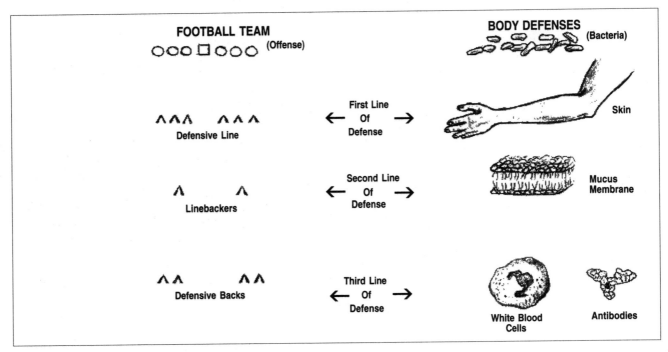

The defensive line and linebackers protect a football team. In a similar way, the skin, mucus membranes, white blood cells, and antibodies protect your body when it is invaded by bacteria. The bacteria is on the offense when it invades.

When you are vaccinated, you are given a small quantity of dead or weakened viruses. In the case of smallpox, these are cowpox or similar viruses. The body reacts to these weakened viruses by producing antibodies which destroy the cowpox viruses. These same antibodies remain in the body and continue to destroy cowpox and smallpox viruses if they enter your body. The antibodies work to make your body immune or resistant to similar diseases for a long time, sometimes your entire life. Sometimes, you need boosters.

How Antibodies Work

(A) Cowpox viruses are injected under the skin. ➡ (B) Viruses cause a blister to develop on the skin.

(C) Body produces antibodies to fight the cowpox viruses. ➡ (D) Cowpox viruses are killed by the antibodies.

(E) Antibodies stay in bloodstream even after the viruses are killed. ➡ (F) If smallpox viruses enter the body, the antibodies kill them quickly.

Dr. Wright spent a great deal of his life attempting to find better treatment procedures and cures for other diseases, too, such as cancer.

If Dr. Wright were living today, he would probably be deeply involved in attempting to find a cure for a disease that affects one out of ten African Americans. The name of that disease is sickle cell anemia.

What is Sickle Cell Anemia?

It has only been in the last twenty years that people have started to find out about sickle cell anemia. Sickle cell anemia is a disease of the blood that mostly affects African Americans.

Diseases That Affect Red Blood Cells

Sickle Cell Anemia	Malaria
trait inherited from parents	plasmodia from the bite of the *Anopheles* mosquito
body produces misshaped red blood cells	plasmodia invade and burst red blood cells
reduces the amount of oxygen the red blood cells can carry through the body	reduces the amount of oxygen the red blood cells can carry through the body
no cure	can usually be cured with such drugs as quinine, chloroquine, and primaquine

The Problems of Sickled Blood Cells

When blood cells are sickled, they are misshaped. They do not move through the bloodstream like normal red blood cells. Because of their shape, they create small blocks in the blood vessels, just like debris that clogs a pipe. The debris keeps the stream from flowing smoothly. The same thing happens in your bloodstream if you have sickled cells. The blood cannot move smoothly. This prevents blood from carrying enough oxygen to the cells.

Normal red blood cells flow freely through a blood vessel. Sickled cells jam the blood vessels so that the blood does not flow freely. (Of course, when a person has sickled cells, they flow throughout the entire heart, not just one part of an artery.)

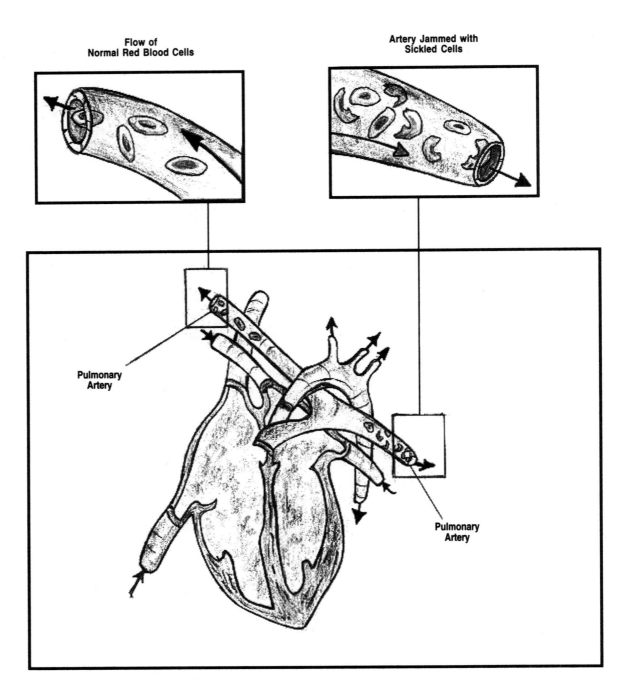

Flow of Normal Red Blood Cells

Artery Jammed with Sickled Cells

Pulmonary Artery

Pulmonary Artery

Sickled cells do not live as long as normal red blood cells. Normal red blood cells live approximately 120 days. Sickled cells live only about 60 days.

Louis Tompkins Wright

1. Review the diseases listed in the chart below. Note the information that needs to be supplied to complete the chart.

2. Research these diseases in your school or public libarary.

3. Complete the chart with the information from the library.

4. Use the chart to complete Hands-On Activity Sheet #2.

Disease Chart

Disease	Definition	Symptoms	Cause	Treatment
Sickle Cell Anemia	Trait that Causes Misshaped Red Blood Cells	Mild or Severe Pain Slow Healing Sores Ulcers Gallstones	Unknown	None
Cancer				
Heart Attack				
Malaria				

Louis Tompkins Wright

Based on information from the disease chart on page 83 and on your research, identify the correct disease from the clue.

1. _____ The disease is caused by sickled cells.

2. _____ African Americans are largely affected by this disease.

3. _____ cured by quinine

4. _____ caused by high blood pressure

5. _____ no known cure for this disease

6. _____ This disease is transmitted by the *Anopheles* mosquito.

7. _____ People who have this disease suffer from severe pain and slow healing sores.

8. _____ There are certain types of this disease treated with x-rays.

Louis Tompkins Wright

You Will Need:

- small box
- slips of paper
- chalk

Play a team quiz game by answering questions about the diseases you have studied in this chapter.

1. Form a team with members of your class.

2. Work with your team members to form questions about different diseases. Write these questions on slips of paper. Write the answers on the backs of these papers.

3. Place the questions in the box.

4. Choose a game host to draw questions from the box. The first team to answer a question correctly earns 10 points. The moderator should keep score on the chalkboard.

5. When all the questions have been answered, tally the scores to determine a winner. The winning team receives the Dr. Louis T. Wright certificate.

Dr. Louis T. Wright Certificate

To _____

For your outstanding work

Signed _____

Teacher

Louis Tompkins Wright

Match the words from the list below with their correct meanings. Write each word on the line by its meaning.

antibodies	Aureomycin	chemotherapy
intradermal technique	malaria	quinine
sickle cell anemia	60 Days	120 Days

_____ 1. the process of giving a person a small quantity of dead or weakened viruses in order to allow the person's body to develop antibodies to fight more dangerous viruses

_____ 2. the substances produced by the human body that help prevent bacteria or virus cells from causing disease

_____ 3. the disease that mainly affects African Americans and causes misshaped red blood cells

_____ 4. the time for which normal red blood cells live

_____ 5. the time for which sickled cells live

_____ 6. the process that is used in the treatment of cancer

_____ 7. an antibiotic that can be used on humans

_____ 8. the disease that is contracted from the bite of the *Anopheles* mosquito, which introduces plasmodia that invade and burst red blood cells

_____ 9. a drug that can cure malaria

GLOSSARY OF TERMS

A

agriculturalist   a scientist who develops better ways to raise crops and livestock

almanac   usually a yearly publication including calendars with weather forecasts, astronomical information and other related information

antibiotic   a drug that stops the growth of bacteria in the body

antibody   the substances produced by the human body that help prevent bacteria and virus cells from causing disease

antiseptic   a chemical used to kill germs

apathy   an expression that lacks emotion

artery   a blood vessel that carries blood away from the heart

astronomer   a person who studies heavenly bodies

atom   the smallest part of an element with the properties of the element

Aureomycin   a drug used to kill bacteria

B

blood bank   a place where blood is stored until it is needed

blood transfusion   the process of taking blood from one person and giving it to another person who needs it

blood type   the kind of blood a person has—A, B, AB, or O

C

capillary   any of the tiny blood vessels that connect the arteries with the veins

carbon monoxide   colorless, odorless, and highly poisonous gas

cell membrane   the thin outer layer of the cytoplasm

chemical energy   energy that can be found, such as the heat energy given off when coal is burned

chemotherapy   a process that is used in the treatment of cancer

coagulation   the condition when blood clots or a small mass of blood is clumped together

corona   the bright light which appears to surround the sun during a total eclipse caused by the moon

cytoplasm   the material in any cell that is between the cell membrane and the nucleus of the cell

E

eclipse   the blocking of one heavenly body by another

ectoplasm   the dense outer part of the cytoplasm

electron   a negative particle that circles the nucleus of an atom

electrogasdynamics channel   a specially designed channel in which electrical energy is produced by the flow of gas

element   one of the basic atoms from which all substances are formed

environment   the living and nonliving things that affect the life of an organism

F

fungus   a life form that is unable to make its own food, so it feeds off others

G

Gulf War   a war fought between the United States and Iraq in the early 1990s

H

heart transplant   a surgery in which one person's damaged heart is replaced with a functioning heart from a willing donor who has just died

hemoglobin   the substance in red blood cells that carries oxygen to the cells

hydroelectric power   the electricity that is produced by water-powered generators

I

interracial   being open or available to people of all races

intradermal technique   the process developed by Dr. Louis Tompkins Wright that eliminated many of the undesirable side effects that can occur when a person is given a vaccination

inventor   one who makes or designs new things

J

Jamaican train **method**   the process of producing sugar by pouring hot sugar cane juice from one kettle to another

K

kinetic energy   energy that is expressed as motion

L

learned behavior   a behavior that an organism is trained to do; not an instinctual or natural behavior

legumes   a family of plants, such as peanuts and beans, that grow seeds in pods

M

malaria   the disease that is contracted from the bite of the *Anopheles* mosquito, which introduces plasmodia that invade and burst red blood cells

mechanical energy   energy produced by machines, such as automobile engines

mold   a type of fungus

molecule   the new substance formed when two or more atoms are combined

mycology   a branch of botany dealing with the study of fungi

N

National Association of Colored People   a group that works for civil rights

NAACP   the abbreviation for the National Association for the Advancement of Colored People

nucleus   1. a rounded bead-like mass of protoplasm that is present in most plant and animal cells 2. the positively charged substance of an atom that is made up of protons and neutrons and around which the electrons circle

neutron   the particle with no charge that is part of the nucleus of an atom

O

osmosis   the process that allows substances to move back and forth through the cell membrane

P

partial eclipse   the partial blocking of one heavenly body by another

penumbra   a partial shadow formed by a heavenly body

plantation   a large estate that is farmed by workers hired by the owner of the land

plasma   the liquid portion of blood; made up of water, dissolved proteins, digested foods, waste products, and minerals

plasmodia   the one-celled animals transferred by the bite of the *Anopheles* mosquito; they invade and burst red blood cells, causing malaria

platelets   the smallest part of the blood; it causes clotting to help stop bleeding

potential energy   stored energy

prevention   the attempt to stop an action from occurring or from occurring in a certain manner

proton   the positive particle that is part of the nucleus of an atom

psychiatrist   a person who is trained as a doctor to treat disorders of the mind

puffball   a large, ball-shaped fungus

quinine   a drug that can cure malaria

R

red blood cells   the part of the blood that transports water, oxygen, food, carbon dioxide, and wastes

response   any reaction to a stimulus

sickle cell anemia   the disease which mainly affects African Americans and that causes misshaped red blood cells

Spingarn Medal   the highest award given by the National Association for the Advancement of Colored People (NAACP)

static electricity   the charges of electricity produced by friction; it is still, not moving or flowing

stethoscope   an instrument that is used to listen to the heart and lungs

stimulus   anything in the environment that causes an organism to react or respond

suffocation   the inability to breathe freely

surveyor   a person who determines the boundaries and areas of land surfaces with the use of certain pieces of equipment

T

total eclipse   the complete blocking of one heavenly body by another

U

umbra   the center of a shadow that blocks all light

unlearned behavior   a behavior that is instinctive or natural, not learned

V

vaccination   the process of giving a person a small quantity of dead or weakened viruses in order to allow the person's body to develop antibodies that fight more dangerous diseases

vacuum pan   the device invented by Norbert Rillieux that replaced the *Jamaican train* method of processing sugar from sugar cane

vein   a blood vessel that carries blood toward the heart

white blood cells   the part of the blood that fights attack by foreign substances

whole blood   the blood that is made up of plasma and blood cells